£1 00

'Of Conscience and Circumstance'

the life of

Rev. William Innes, D.D.

1770-1885

in the context of his times

with best wishes

Amanda Bruce

Amanda Bruce

Published by
Canonmills Press
Edinburgh 2010

This text was written and submitted for the degree of Master of Theology at New College, Divinity Faculty, University of Edinburgh, 2003 and was revised and published to coincide with the Bi-Centenary of the congregation of Canonmills Church, Edinburgh, 2010.

ISBN 978-0-9566956-0-4

Printed by Prontaprint Ltd. Edinburgh

Front Cover: Rev. William Innes, D.D.

Back Cover: The grave of William Innes who is buried in the grounds of St.Cuthbert's Parish, Edinburgh – the stone was erected by the congregation of Elder Street Chapel.

for the Canonmills Family

INTRODUCTION

"I know, and all the world knows, that revolutions never go backward"
WILLIAM HENRY SEWARD

The life of William Innes stretched for almost eighty-five years and did so across two centuries. During that time the world in which he lived was fast changing. Socially, politically, culturally, there was flux and while this proved to be of concern to many, for others it was an exciting time in which to be living and working.

Innes was born in 1770 and during the first half of his life the Western world was wrought with political agitation, war and the threat of war. The single most important event at the end of the eighteenth century was the French Revolution. The fervour out of which the Revolution was born and that which it created impacted on and radically coloured all areas of life for some time to come. Suddenly, authoritarian structures which had seemed so indestructible were proven to be fallible. In Britain the government and the established churches felt particularly threatened by these developments, both being examples of institutions to which hierarchical power structures were fundamental.

Scotland's national church was in the grip of Moderatism during the first decades of Innes' life. The moderate party was opposed to its evangelical rival which it considered a challenge to its authority. Evangelical theology was founded on the authority of the gospel and criticised the fact that the moderates tried to impose their interpretation of Christianity on to people. By the time William Innes was born, dissatisfaction was already obvious within the Church of Scotland. In 1770 there were more than two hundred Seceder congregations in existence. During the 1790s, with the call for liberty, freedom of choice, and personal religion in the air, those who had a mind for dissent were encouraged in their campaigns while the people of Scotland were more likely to defy the ecclesiastical establishment and give time to those preaching the gospel outwith the church in which they had grown up.

Whenever ground shifts it is inevitable that some structures and models will be destabilised, either falling away or rendering themselves needful of renovation. However, 'groundswells' also provide the foundations for new ventures. William Innes was one of those men of his generation who took advantage of the social and political circumstances of his day, almost subconsciously responding to the opportunities for change which were continually presented to him. Several of his friends and contemporaries are known for the part they played in changing the face of religious life in Scotland – James Alexander Haldane, his brother Robert and Greville Ewing, to mention but three. Indeed, their influence on Innes was significant. But Innes' influence on

1

them has yet to be recorded, as has his part in quietly but substantially influencing debate on several theological issues, most extensively in the areas of baptism, church union and forbearance.

The circumstances of the age in which Innes lived, combined with his deeply held conviction that individuals be accountable for their beliefs and actions at any given time, shaped his life and his work and characterised his ministry. As Innes' thought matured and his theology developed, his position in and involvement with an institutional church shifted. Within twelve years, Innes had moved from ministering under the rule of the established church to leading a small congregation of seventeen people in rented accommodation with a most liberal constitution for the time of its founding. That congregation survives today as Canonmills Church, Edinburgh; still an unique church for its time, influenced in part by the principles which William Innes accepted for himself and sought to instil in others.

CHAPTER I
CONFORMING AND CONFESSING

"...With my childhood's faith..."
ROBERT BROWNING

It can be said he was a man like any other - a web of contradictions. And yet these gave him an unique character, highly respected and well loved by friends, contemporaries and opponents alike. For many years a devoted parish minister of the established Church of Scotland he was, for many more, an independent, Congregationalist, Baptist minister; a biblical fundamentalist yet a revolutionary spirit who displayed a remarkable openness to the opinions and beliefs of others; a man who valued conscience, principles and duty yet a risk-taker, prepared to walk in new and unknown ways. His was to be a life of constant questioning. This is not to say he did not hold strong beliefs – he did – but these beliefs were never inscrutable. He was a man of questions because his was a life of faith.

****

William Innes was born a 'son of the manse' on the 31st of March, 1770. Three years previously, Mary Hogg of Edinburgh, moved to the parish of Gifford in Haddingtonshire to marry James Innes, minister of the established Church of Scotland in the parish of Yester. William was the second of five children to be born to the couple although they were to see only two of them survive into adulthood – William and his youngest sister, Anne.

It seemed inevitable that ministry would shape Innes' life, having being born into a family whose last two generations had seen this as their vocation, his father's father (also James) being the parish minister of Mertoun in the Scottish borders. James senior (Innes' grandfather), educated at the University of Edinburgh, then known as 'the College' (from 'Collegium Jacobi Sexti'), was first rector of the Grammar School in Hawick before becoming ordained into the Presbytery of Jedburgh. He would pride himself on the education of his family and his mixture of formal teaching by book and practical teaching by example filtered through the generations, to James junior (Innes' father) and to William himself.

For William Innes, as for all children born and baptised to Presbyterian parents in eighteenth century Scotland, fidelity to the Kirk was all but unquestioned. Loyalty to one's father's church may have been instilled as a virtue by the church itself, but a virtue it was still considered. As Innes would discover later in his life, the thought that anyone might challenge the institution was met with a tone of parental disappointment and angry frustration in the face of wilful 'disobedience'. In the 'fatherly admonition' that would be set out against Innes and his evangelical contemporaries in 1799, the General Assembly of the Church of Scotland asked,

> Is it to be imagined, that any well-disposed and sober-minded Christians could think of deserting those houses of God, in which their fathers have so often worshipped? ... Is not the Church of Scotland, which has been distinguished by the testimony of many generations for the purity of its doctrines, and the character of its ministries, worthy of your most steady and zealous attachment; that Church, in defence of which your forefathers fought and bled...? ... Listen not to any insinuations from those who seek to pervert you from the sound and good principles you early imbibed...[1]

For the young Innes, however, obedience to God and to the established Church were still synonymous.

It was at the age of fourteen that Innes decided to follow his father and grandfather before him and train for the ministry, (fourteen, for he was ordained in his twenty-fourth year after studying and serving a probationary appointment for a statutory nine-year period.[2])

In the years preceding this, Innes had received his schooling under the watch of private tutors. His parents fostered in him a streak of independence from an early age, sending him into Edinburgh to take his lessons. For more than a year (1782-1783) he spent one hour a day under the tutelage of James Mitchell, a "strict Presbyterian"[3] employed by the father of the future author, Walter Scott, for his son. Together they had lessons in French, studied themes in the classics and "acquired ... knowledge of school-divinity and church-history, and a great acquaintance in particular with the old books describing the early history of the Church of Scotland, the wars and sufferings of the Covenanters, and so forth."[4] As Innes notes, studying with Scott "created no small degree of intimacy. Though afterwards we were engaged in different pursuits, he studying for the Scottish bar, and I for the Scottish Church, I always found him of the same affable and agreeable disposition by which he was distinguished in his early days."[5] Sir Walter Scott was only one of the notable men whom circumstances brought together with William Innes. However, in later years he declined to enter into correspondence with his friend on theological matters.[6]

While still of schooling years, Innes lodged for some time with a Methodist preacher. Dr. Hamilton is the only man outside the family who is recorded as

---

[1] -----, Acts of the General Assembly of The Church of Scotland 1638 – 1842 (Edinburgh, 1834), p.871-2
[2] see A.C. Thomas, Dr Innes and His Times (Edinburgh, 1855), p.16
[3] J. Sutherland, The Life of Walter Scott (Oxford, 1997), p.22
[4] D. Daiches, Sir Walter Scott and his world (Norwich, 1971), p.29
[5] W. Innes, Suggestions for Thoughtful but Sceptical Minds (Edinburgh, 1854), p.57
[6] letter from Sir. Walter Scott to Rev. William Innes, dated London, 19th April, 1828, cited in W. Innes (ibid.)

having influenced the young man in his decision to devote his life to the church. Innes had a great respect for his landlord and he was moved by the familial way in which Hamilton considered him. He was, it is said, "forcibly arrested by the good man praying for him and other members of the family by name."[7] Innes was always to value personal piety.

On the 27th of March, 1792, Innes was licensed by the Presbytery of Haddington. The following year he found patronage with the local magistrates and was duly elected on the 9th of May. Three months later, on the 15th of August and at the age of twenty-three, Innes was ordained as a minister of the established Church of Scotland, subscribing to The Scots Confession of 1560 and embracing the legal undertakings of the Presbyterian system of church government he would soon reject.

On the day of his ordination, Innes was admitted to the second charge of Stirling East parish church, as colleague and successor to Rev. James Somerville, later D.D.. The parish comprised the market burgh of Stirling itself, along with two villages, Raploch and Abbey, providing Innes with a wide pastoral responsibility. In addition to this, the second charge carried with it the duty of being Chaplain to Stirling Castle by Commission of H.M. King George III. William Innes was well respected in the parish, and could preach to capacity congregations of almost two thousand at a time. The Reverends Somerville and Innes were considered to be "pious and learned"; Mr Somerville, "eminent for his masculine turn of thought and decision of character"; and Mr. Innes, "whose agreeable conversation, pleasing manners, and attractive style of preaching, added weight to the influence of his consistent character and genuine Christianity."[8]

Having witnessed and having heard recounted the paths the lives of his father and grandfather had taken before him, William Innes would have been well aware of the prospects of his future in Stirling. As was noted some time after his death by the Rev. Jonathan Watson of Edinburgh, "He was settled in one of the most pleasant and lucrative positions he could have enjoyed as minister of Stirling. Highly respected and greatly beloved, a course of comparatively easy and useful years lay before him as a country parish minister, which many might have envied."[9]

Innes' conscience, however, was not to let him sit securely and comfortably in his post. Disillusionment with the workings of the Church of Scotland was quick to bed itself in his mind and Innes' childhood faith in the

---

[7] A.C.Thomas, Dr Innes and His Times (Edinburgh, 1855), p.16
[8] A. Haldane, The Lives of Robert Haldane of Airthrey, and of his Brother, James Alexander Haldane Esq. (London, 1853), p.94
[9] Cited: A. Baines History of Dublin Street Baptist Church, Edinburgh 1885-1958 (Edinburgh, 1958), p. 23

established church, though not in God or the Christian religion, was to be severely shaken.

CHAPTER II
SEPARATION

"Give me the liberty to know, to utter and to argue freely
according to conscience above all other liberties"
JOHN MILTON

William Innes remained Second Minister of East Church, Stirling, for just over six years. It was not until 1804, five years after his disassociation with the established church, that he published in a series of letters his <u>Reasons for Separating from the Church of Scotland</u>. Partly this was to satisfy those of his contemporaries who constantly questioned his decision, but also, to take the opportunity to justify that decision, while expressing his remaining affection for those former colleagues who remained within the system he could no longer abide.

Innes additionally confessed that he had found it extremely difficult to face up to his growing dissatisfaction with Presbyterian church government. "I recollect well," he says, "the time...when I felt it extremely unpleasant to hear such a subject introduced,"[10] and, although he says "I secretly felt difficulties from my connexion (sic) to the establishment," discussions with respected friends and "the general consideration of my occupying a sphere of extensive usefulness, if it did not remove them altogether, helped me, for a time at least, to banish them from my thoughts."[11] Suppressing his concerns for a time, Innes was much admired by his parishioners for both his preaching and his congenial nature.

He made several close associations, some of which served to determine the path his life would take in years to come. Through his chaplaincy to the Forces, Innes met James Alexander Haldane. James had married the daughter of the Deputy Governor of Stirling Castle. It was not long before he introduced to Innes his brother Robert who at that time owned the nearby estate of Airthrey. The two Haldane brothers became close friends; Robert, especially, would invite Innes to his home where they would converse late into the evenings. It was during one of these meetings that Innes sparked off Robert's interest in worship through his suggestion that they should end their evening with prayers. Haldane was moved by this experience as Innes had similarly been moved by the prayers of his Edinburgh landlord some years before. The next evening, Robert introduced a period of bible reading and prayer as a formal part of the nightly regime in his home.[12] Some time later, Innes would also introduce Robert to

---

[10] W. Innes, "Letter I" <u>Reasons for Separating from The Church of Scotland</u> (Dundee, 1804), p.2
[11] W. Innes, (ibid.)
[12] Cited: A. Haldane, <u>The Lives of Robert Haldane of Airthrey, and of his Brother, James Alexander Haldane Esq.</u> (London,1853) p.95

7

William Carey's pioneering missionary work in India, this being the catalyst for Robert taking up the cause of spreading the Gospel.

Settled in Stirling, Innes married his cousin Jean, the daughter of his uncle, Dr. Robert Innes of Giffordvale. They began a family, and an assured income seemed eminently sensible. All the while, however, Innes was becoming more hostile to the established church and began seriously to question the tenability of his position. That one should be loyal to one's church was, as we have seen, deeply engrained in Innes and he records on more than one occasion that he sought in his enquiries to find sound principles on which to base his decision to remain a parish minister. "If I had any bias," he remarked later, "it was in favour of my continuing in habits of professional intercourse with many valuable friends..."[13]

The catalyst for William Innes' split with the Church of Scotland came in the last year of the nineteenth century. In his <u>Hints on Church Government from the Experience of Above Half a Century</u>, Innes reflects objectively on what happened:

> When I was minister of Stirling a vacancy occurred in the presbytery. A preacher was presented by the patron to the charge. It may be necessary to mention that, according to Presbyterian forms, a service called 'serving the edict' is appointed to take place in the church of the vacant parish where the presbytery meet and the parishioners after sermon are asked if they have any objections to the life or doctrine of the presentee. On this occasion one of the parishioners came forward and said, we have; we are prepared to prove that he is guilty of profane swearing. This service had so far degenerated into a mere form that the presbytery were taken by surprise. They felt, however, that they were bound to enquire what proof there was to establish the above charge. The presentee, aware of what was to take place, had his law agent present, who took a protest and appealed to the synod. The presbytery was thus dragged first to the synod and then to the General Assembly. It was there pleaded that we should either give up such a form or follow it out, and not insult the common sense of mankind, by asking a question and then virtually say that no reply was to be heard. What is called the moderate party had the majority. They accordingly enacted that, without any inquiry, the presbytery should assemble on a certain day and ordain the presentee, according to the rules of the church. Nay it was further ordained that *all* the presbytery should be present however much opposed to their convictions, though this was not necessary, and not required on other occasions. This was intended as a punishment to the refractory members, or, as Mr. Rowland Hill expressed it, to "stretch their consciences, which were a little too tight". This (was) a strong case but it best illustrates the nature of the power. The power was *there* and it is the existence of such power I condemn as opposed to some of the first principles of the oracles of. God.[14]

---

[13] W. Innes, "Letter III" <u>Reasons for Separating from The Church of Scotland</u> (Dundee, 1804), p.28
[14] W. Innes, <u>Hints on Church Government</u> (Edinburgh, 1852), pp. 27-9

Thus, it was the system of government and the legality of the church, combined with the fact that the people of the parish were being 'lorded over', which forced his hand; it was the *power* of Presbyterianism and the authority which he saw men claim where it was not their right to claim it. That the church should have only one 'head', he had pledged on the occasion of his ordination by his subscription to 'The Scots Confession'. In action, however, he experienced at first hand the way in which the Church of Scotland invested too great an authority in their man-made councils and this he could not stomach.

More generally, it was firstly its constitution and secondly its system of administration which induced Innes to relinquish his connection with the established church. It was a matter for his conscience and he insists his move "was not the result of a hasty decision."[15]

Innes had long been interested in the missionary work that was taking place internationally at the time. The reception of the pamphlet on Carey's journeys in India compounded this and when he had shown it to Robert Haldane it was proposed that a tour be made in a similar vein to that of their mentor. Innes was keen to embark on the voyage but their plans were thwarted by the East India Company who refused permission for missionaries to enter the country and withheld any hope of funding the venture. The year was 1796 and the two Haldane brothers had by this time seriously taken up the challenge of ministry as they defined it. This was not to embark on a process which would lead to their ordination. Rather, they would become, what the established church termed derogatorily, 'lay preachers'. This, as the Haldanes perceived it, was to take up the challenge of being a Christian in the world; to take the Gospel to all who would listen.

It was suggested to Innes that he should join their venture more seriously than simply accompanying them on their tours. "I recollect well," says Innes, "when the proposition was made to me to leave my charge and occupy another station unconnected with the establishment, the idea that first occurred to my mind was that I should feel very great reluctance in accepting it. Our enquiries, however, are frequently suggested by our circumstances...(and) the difficulties I had often experienced led me to consider this proposal as a call to engage in as full an investigation of the subject as possible, that in the issue I might either remain in it without uneasiness, or, from a conviction of duty, deliberately relinquish it."[16]

In his enquiry, Innes works from the premise, "That church is most likely to prosper, which, in the form of its government, comes nearest the model, or is most agreeable to the principles which Christ, either during his personal ministry, or afterwards through the medium of his Apostles, hath made known to us in his word."[17] Further, as far as he can discern from his study of the New Testament,

---

[15] W. Innes, "Letter III" <u>Reasons for Separating from The Church of Scotland</u> (Dundee, 1804), p.27
[16] W. Innes, (ibid.), pp. 27-8
[17] W. Innes, "Letter I" <u>Reasons for Separating from The Church of Scotland</u> (Dundee, 1804), p. 10

Presbyterianism is "completely unscriptural."[18] Being a representational form of government, Presbyterianism fails to recognise the corporate element of the body of Christ; the 'Laos', the laity – or 'the people of God' – whom Innes regards as the Church in its true sense. Innes believes that Presbyterianism denies the individuals who make up the church the responsibility which is demanded of each of them to know their own minds. In the case of church discipline, for example, the people had no say and were rarely informed of the principles on which decisions were based. Citing the use of the word 'church' in scripture he observes, "In no case does it seem employed to denote the rulers of a church, as distinguished from the general body."[19]

To conclude his argument, Innes criticises the example of the synod of Jerusalem (as set out in Acts, chapter xv) which is said to be an example of a court of reference or appeal and is given as evidence that Presbyterianism was founded by the Apostles. The Synod of Jerusalem was unique, Innes asserts, because of the presence of the Apostles in the church. The Apostles being appointed to regulate everything concerning the Christian Church, it was natural that their opinion should be consulted under the various opinions that existed in the church at Antioch. Their authority, however, should not be assumed by any minister of the established church. Innes says,

> I hold then that no body of men is entitled to claim obedience to their decrees as the Apostles did to theirs. Let presbyteries be held as a matter of expediency, and as useful for mutual advice, and no one can object to them. But...(let them not) exercise authority...[20]

Circumstances and conscience combined to allow Innes to accept that his dissociation with the Church of Scotland was to be formal. Surrounded by likeminded contemporaries and with the zeal to take on the challenge of ministry outwith the establishment at a time when more people were likely to take such a movement seriously, the prospect of moving away from all that he had known and grown up with became feasible. Indeed, it was the only option possible. Once events in Stirling came to a head, Innes knew his conscience would no longer allow him to remain in his charge. The attitude of the Church Courts, together with the results of his studies, persuaded him that to do so would be hypocritical. It was presumably, then, with a mixture of sadness and relief that on 8th October, 1799, he was finally libelled and deposed by the General Assembly of the Church of Scotland.

William Innes had gained his liberty. But at what cost to himself and his young family?

---

[18] W. Innes, "Letter III" (ibid.), p.28
[19] W. Innes, (ibid.), p.34
[20] W. Innes, Hints on Church Government from the experience of above half a century (Edinburgh, 1852), p.26

CHAPTER III
REVOLUTIONS AND RESOLUTIONS

"The music of the Gospel leads us home"
FREDERICK WILLIAM FABER

"We hold these truths to be sacred and undeniable;
that all men are created equal and independent."
THOMAS JEFFERSON

Within the two decades before Innes' birth both the first Baptist Church and the first Paedobaptist Independent Church in Scotland were formed; the former, Keiss Church in Caithness, the latter in Glasgow. The 'campaign for ecclesiastical democracy' – the move to abolish patronage – had been grumbling on, although there was little sign of reform being achieved.

Thirty years later the mood for independence was heightened. Thomas Paine's Rights of Man had been published in 1792 and was widely distributed and easily available. Arguably, Kant's Critique of Pure Reason (1782) and, in Scotland especially, the writings of David Hume[21] had previously undermined the rationalist philosophy which had fostered Moderatism. All the while, the contemporary situation was being reported on and disseminated amongst a higher percentage of the population than ever before as the number of newspapers increased considerably. The social and political consciousness of ordinary folk was stirred and questions surrounding the nature and expression of authority were being raised. Not only was there a heightened awareness among the masses that they had rights, there was a growing impetus to fight for them. The rising tide of such awareness had been felt earlier in the century with the arguments for burgh reform and the abolition of patronage within the church, but it was the French Revolution of 1789 which, at the very least, had "greatly aggravated (this) climate of tension, suspicion, grievance and unrest."[22]

In the context of religion, the response to this mood was expressed in the upsurge of interest in missionary work and evangelical Christianity. This was immediately interpreted as a dangerous and subversive movement by the vulnerable churchmen of the establishment. As Emma Vincent points out, "Liberty and equality, as demanded by the radicals, were frightening concepts to most

---

[21] "We may conclude, that the Christian religion not only was at first attended by miracles, but even at this day cannot be believed by any reasonable person without one. Mere reason is insufficient to convince us of its veracity; And whoever is moved by faith to assent to it, is conscious of a continued miracle in his own person..." David Hume, Natural History of Religion (1757) Cf. Dialogues Concerning Natural Religion (1779)

[22] E.Vincent, "The Responses of Scottish Churchmen to the French Revolution, 1789 – 1802" (1994), p.193

ministers."[23] Along with the Government, the Church of Scotland was a dominant voice in the control of national life. Any hint of anarchy was seen as a threat to this position of power. Vincent goes on to discuss the political preaching that was part of the conservative response of the established church to events in France. From a study of a wide spectrum of sermons she discerns a commonality: "They argued that religion was not in fact separate from politics: since God was at work in society, religion was essential in order to please Him and to obtain His favour for political activities."[24]

Thus, through a fear for its own stability, the Kirk allied itself with the Government in an attempt to parallel the emergence of the evangelical party with the barbarous French freedom fighters. They argued that evangelicals were working to encourage their countrymen to rise against the laws of the land and that doing such could only be frightful, dangerous and corrupt. Practically, Church of Scotland ministers sought to suppress those who were zealously responding to the emerging climate of freedom and responsibility. Foreign mission was frowned upon and itinerant preachers lambasted as opportunists with no scruples, who cared only to make a name for themselves.

It was against this backdrop that the likes of Robert and James Haldane, William Innes and his then brother-in-law Greville Ewing took up the evangelical cause of promoting the 'kingdom'. These men knew where their priorities lay. Robert Haldane spoke for his contemporary allies as much as for himself when he stated, "Christianity is everything or nothing. If it be true, it warrants and commands every sacrifice to promote its influence. If it be not, then let us lay aside the hypocrisy of professing to believe it."[25]

In 1796, having been inspired by Carey's[26] first periodical accounts of the Baptist Mission in India, passed on to him by Innes, Robert Haldane of Airthrey became deeply impressed with the possibilities for taking the message of the gospel to 'heathens' abroad and set about arranging a mission to Bengal with Innes and Ewing as proposed travelling companions. Despite being forbidden to go ahead by the East India Company, their intended journey was one of several proposed missions which, along with the founding of the Edinburgh Missionary Society, raised concerns within the Church of Scotland. As J. H. S. Burleigh points out in his Church History of Scotland, "the Presbyterian system with its insistence on parochial ministrations did not offer a kindly welcome to itinerant evangelists, even when they were its own children"[27] and, as such, the General Assembly of 1796 refused all support of foreign mission.[28] However, it was their justification

---

[23] E. Vincent, (ibid.), p.198
[24] E. Vincent (ibid.), p.196
[25] A. Haldane, The Lives of Robert Haldane of Airthrey, and of his Brother, James Alexander Haldane Esq. (London, 1853), p.98
[26] William Carey, founder of the Baptist Missionary Society 1793
[27] J.H.S. Burleigh, A Church History of Scotland OUP (London, 1960), p.311
[28] " It was argued that the Gospel could be preached only to the civilized, that missionary societies were supported by people from different denominations, that they would export sectarianism and that they were associated with radical political elements and agitation against the slave trade; so the Assembly

for this ruling which led to the success of the evangelists. "There were enough heathens in Scotland that one should not be concerned with reaching those abroad," declared the Assembly. It took little time for the evangelists' response of turning their attentions to promoting the Gospel at home.

Domestic missions had to rely on the sponsorship of the Relief Church and from the Haldane brothers themselves. Robert decided in 1796 to sell his paternal estate and, although the sale did not come through for two years, he drew considerable amounts from letting the land of the estate and that which he owned in Forfarshire. 1796 also saw Robert's brother James embark on a missionary tour of the Scottish Highlands accompanied by Charles Simeon of Cambridge with the purpose of distributing religious tracts. A lay preacher, J.A. Haldane soon drew large crowds as his brother and contemporaries were also to do.

From July of the same year, Greville Ewing and Charles Stuart published the *Missionary Magazine*, an interdenominational journal filled with accounts of domestic missions and tracts. With a circulation of five or six thousand, the Edinburgh magazine brought together a considerable body of people who supported the reason for its existence; "to excite and to guide the zeal...by disseminating all the information which they can procure respecting attempts to propagate the Gospel of Jesus Christ."[29] It was "a periodical ... intended as a repository of discussion and intelligence respecting the progress of the Gospel"[30] and its publication was seen in the same way as the various missionary societies formed in England and Scotland; as a war cry against the Kirk from "irrational sources beyond their control."[31]

William Innes was a subscriber to the *Missionary Magazine* and while still a minister of the Church of Scotland also supported what was "a more permanent commitment to lay evangelism"[32] the 'Society for the Propagation of the Gospel at Home'. The Society, created in December 1797, was one of equals under the direction of twelve laymen led by James Haldane who rejected the term 'laity' as a "popish distinction."[33] The Society was a non-sectarian and inter-denominational body designed to promote preaching and catechising, to "make known the everlasting Gospel of our Lord Jesus Christ"[34] and to support itinerants as they

---

dismissed the appeal." W.D. McNaughton, "A Few Historical Notes on Scottish Congregationalism" http://www.westendcongregationalchurch.org/congregation.htm, p.1

[29] G. Ewing Ed., *Missionary Magazine* Vol. I, No.i: Jul 1796, p.i

[30] Ewing (ibid.) Mission Statement as of Title Page.

[31] E. Vincent, "The Responses of Scottish Churchmen to the French Revolution, 1789 – 1802" (1994), p.203

[32] D. Lovegrove, "Lay leadership, establishment crisis and the disdain of the clergy" in The Rise of the Laity in Evangelical Protestantism (London & New York, 2002), p.121

[33] J.A. Haldane, Journal of a Tour (----,1798), p.5

[34] G. Ewing Ed., *Missionary Magazine* (----,1798), p.58; Cited in W.D. McNaughton, "A Few Historical Notes on Scottish Congregationalism" http://www.westendcongregationalchurch.org/congregation.htm, p.3

toured from the cities to the remotest parts of the Scottish countryside "promoting pure and undefiled religion."[35]

It was not until 1799 that William Innes would eventually join Robert Haldane on a tour of the North. Haldane had, by this time, already undertaken the pastoral care of the Circus Church in Edinburgh but had done so on the proviso that "this should not prevent his labouring as an evangelist in the highways and hedges."[36] Mr. Aikman, a friend to both Innes and Haldane joined the party and, between them, their tour took them from Dundee to Arbroath, Lawrencekirk, Aberdeen, Banff, Huntly, Elgin, Forres, Inverness, Wick, Thurso, Kirkwall, Fair Isle, Lerwick, and North Maven. In Shetland, the Haldanes' biographer and descendant records that the development of religious life had been directly traced to the preaching of Robert Haldane and Innes: "Their earnest and rousing addresses broke in upon the dangerous repose of the people, exciting a spirit of inquiry there before unknown, when, by the blessing of God, not a few were turned to righteousness."[37] During the time of this tour, there occurred one of the most notorious meetings of the General Assembly of the Church of Scotland. While in England, as Deryck Lovegrove notes, "the clerical reaction to the upsurge of lay preaching, though sharp and outspoken, was largely confined to polemics...", in Scotland, "the more centralised character of the established church produced a more concerted reaction"[38] and it was at the 1799 Assembly that this reaction was publicly declared.

On May, 28th a *Declaratory Act of the General Assembly of the Church of Scotland, respecting Unqualified Ministers and Preachers* was issued, followed closely on June 3rd by a *Pastoral Admonition, addressed by the General Assembly of the Church of Scotland...to all the People under their Charge.* The former of these declarations condemned those who had received no ordination, those who received ordination out-with the bounds of the Kirk and those who had forfeited their licence through their associations with lay preachers. William Innes clearly fell into the final category. When he officially resigned his charge, a complaint was raised against him as the Kirk did not want to be seen to be losing its ministers to the 'opposition'. Innes was formally ordered to return to Stirling and it was only on his refusal to do so that the Church of Scotland was happy to libel and depose him. It should be remembered, too, that the Haldanes and Ewing had all begun their Evangelical work as members of the Kirk and only renounced their membership as late as 1798 under the pressure of increasing hostility. As it has been said, "In relation to the dominant Presbyterianism, the new evangelical

---

[35] - - - - -, An Account of the Proceedings of The Society for Propagating the Gospel at Home (Edinburgh, 1799), p.58

[36] A. Haldane, The Lives of Robert Haldane of Airthrey, and of his Brother, James Alexander Haldane Esq. (London, 1853), p.262

[37] Kinniburgh Historical Survey p,55 cited A. Haldane (ibid.), p. 269

[38] D. Lovegrove, "Lay leadership, establishment crisis and the disdain of the clergy" in The Rise of the Laity in Evangelical Protestantism (London & New York, 2002), p.121

departure was a case of 'coming out from among them.' "[39] These words from the declaration of May 28th show clearly why this had to be the case.

> The General Assembly, considering that it is of the greatest importance to the interests of true religion, to the sound instruction of the people, to the quiet of their minds, and the peace of the Church and State, that unqualified persons, who intrude themselves into the ministry of the Word, shall not receive any countenance from ministers of this Church; more especially in the present times, when men, who avow their hostility to our ecclesiastical establishment, and their contempt of all the rules which the wisdom of our ancestors framed upon the model of Scripture, for the orderly dispensation of the word and sacraments, are traversing all the districts within the bounds of this Church, and attempting to alienate the minds of the people from their established teachers; considering also, that it is essential to the unity and good order of the Church, and implied in the fundamental principles of Presbyterian government, that no minister shall presume to set up his individual judgement in opposition to the judgement of those to whom, at his ordination he promised subjection in the Lord...do hereby discharge and prohibit...all the ministers of this church...from employing to preach upon any occasion, or to dispense any of the other ordinances of the Gospel, within any congregation under the jurisdiction of this Church, persons who are not qualified, according to the laws of this Church, to accept of a presentation, and from holding ministerial communion in any other manner with such persons.[40]

The message of the *Pastoral Admonition* runs along the same lines but is addressed to all the members of the Church and was issued as a statement to be read from every pulpit across the land. As such, it warns of the dangers of listening to itinerants, urging loyalty to the established church on the pain of censure. The *Pastoral Admonition* attacks the legitimacy of the independent evangelists by likening their ventures to those of the political radicals who instigated bloody rebellion and anarchy on the continent.

To some extent the fear of their ministers being undermined was justified as it had been common for the itinerants to visit a parish church on a Sunday morning and in the evening preach in the town centre or its equivalent, criticising the minister they had heard. However, this practice had been rejected as unhelpful to their cause since the summer of 1797. William Innes was concerned to make it clear that the aim of evangelical independent preachers was not to take issue with ordained ministers of the Church of Scotland; after all, he had been one for seven years and loved and respected many of his former colleagues:

> Let no one here insinuate we wish to alienate your affections from your ministers. No, brethren; but you yourselves will allow, that great as that

---

[39] Hon Lord Sands, "The Historical Origins of the Religious Divisions in Scotland" (1929), p.86
[40] - - - - -, Acts of the General Assembly of The Church of Scotland 1638 – 1842 (Edinburgh, 1843), p.869

ought to be for their works sake, and the truth that dwelleth in them, your attachment to the cause of the Lord Jesus ought to be much greater[41].

The other main attack of the Kirk – the itinerants' supposed political involvement – was vigorously denied. There was only one instance of a political speech, delivered by Robert Haldane a full seven years before the allegations were made. In addition to this, in a reply to the Admonition, Rowland Hill[42] was able to point to the rules of the Society of the Propagation of the Gospel at Home which explicitly forbade its members to comment on political issues. Lovegrove picks up on the fact that "Hill implied that the General Assembly had used the political smear as a tactical device for hitting back at a movement that posed a challenge to its religious control"[43].

The Kirk indeed "betrayed a strong sense of professional jealousy"[44] by their scathing remarks against the 'uneducated' and 'unqualified' laity having no authority to preach the gospel. To these comments, however, their opponents simply rejoined by pointing out that Christ, Himself, had been a lay preacher.

Five months after the 1799 meeting of the General Assembly, William Innes found himself in the same position as the Haldanes and Ewing. He was no longer a part of the established church and so was able officially to align himself with the independent evangelical preachers who, despite the best efforts of the Church of Scotland, were to rise to great prominence by the turn of the century. Their appeal was partly derived from the principles and beliefs they championed and their approach to spreading the gospel which engaged so many who heard them, but it was also partly due to the circumstances of time and place in which they put their beliefs into practice. The rise of the 'Haldane Movement' as it has become known, happened to come at a time when among the general public there was, as Drummond and Bulloch point out, "a rising dissatisfaction with a clerically organized church."[45]

Their personal integrity and conduct must also have at least played a part in determining the success they met with. The impression of one visitor from England, Mr Andrew Fuller, who preached in the Circus Church in Edinburgh, was that, "These appear to be excellent men, free from the extravagance and nonsense which infect some. They appear...very intelligent, serious and affectionate in their

---

[41] W. Innes, "Letter VI" Reasons for Separating from The Church of Scotland (Dundee, 1804), p.90
[42] Rowland Hill (1744-1833) itinerant preacher who had been refused priest's orders. He was an ordained deacon of the Church of England but chose to found his own church, building Surrey Chapel, Blackfriars Road, London in 1783.
[43] D. Lovegrove, "Lay leadership, establishment crisis and the disdain of the clergy" in The Rise of the Laity in Evangelical Protestantism (London & New York, 2002), p.129; cf. R. Hill, "A Series of Letters Occasioned by the Late Pastoral Admonition of the Church of Scotland..." (Edinburgh, 1799), pp. 8-14
[44] D. Lovegrove (ibid.), p.125
[45] A. Drummond & J. Bulloch, The Scottish Church 1688 – 1843 (Edinburgh, 1973), p.153

work; active, liberal...no drollery in their preaching, but very desirous to be and do everything that is right."[46]

It was no surprise, then, that when the Haldanes founded the Tabernacle Churches across Scotland they were soon popular meeting places for Christian worship. William Innes was proud to find himself pastor to two of these congregations and became a vocal supporter of the principles on which they were founded.

---

[46] In a letter of *October 1799* from Mr. Andrew Fuller, cited in A. Haldane, The Lives of Robert Haldane of Airthrey, and of his Brother, James Alexander (London, 1853), p.229; Cf. J.Ross, A History of Congregational Independency in Scotland (Glasgow, 1900), p. 53

CHAPTER IV
RESPONSIBLE CHRISTIANITY

"The first of earthly blessings, independence"
EDWARD GIBBON

The precursor to the Tabernacle venture had been the Edinburgh 'Circus' in Little King Street. The building which had formerly been a variety theatre was transformed into a place of worship and the 'Circus' was formally constituted in the January of 1799 – due to the strong personal convictions of Greville Ewing – on congregational principles. The Circus drew many visitors and preachers from England including Rowland Hill who was present at its opening. These visitors were to become close friends of the Tabernacles which were first established in Glasgow, Dundee, Perth, Elgin and Caithness.

William Innes first became personally involved with the Congregational Church when he accepted the call to become the pastor of the Tabernacle in Dundee. Having a wife and, by this stage, two young children to support, he waited a full year to carefully consider his position before taking up the appointment on the 19th of October, 1800. As Kirkland discusses, there was no hierarchy allowed within these 'churches'. Functional distinctions were permitted but otherwise all believers were placed on the same level,[47] and this independent form of church government appealed especially to Innes.

Congregationalism embraced the involvement of each member and encouraged every person to think for themselves about their Christian faith. "Wherever Christianity exists," argues Innes, "it will in a certain degree tend to improve the morals of a people...But that improvement is the result of those valuable principles contained in Christianity being made known, not of the circumstance of its being by law established."[48] Thus, Innes believes that whatever principles and beliefs are preached or heard or read about, it is the responsibility of each individual who professes to be a Christian to discover his position in relation to these and to then put what he believes to be true into practice in his everyday life. "Each of us...should be solicitous to improve to the utmost possible degree every opportunity of usefulness,"[49] he wrote.

Standing outwith the bounds of the Kirk, Innes was able to write and speak publicly on his concerns anent Presbyterian Church Government: "As the Presbyterian system claims a right on behalf of the majority of the congregations in a Presbytery, to exercise authority over any of their number, and to require

---

[47] Paraphrased from an account of church government as instituted by J.A. Haldane. See W. Kirkland, "The Impact of the French Revolution on Scottish Religious Life and Thought..." *Degree of Doctor of Philosophy* (University of Edinburgh, 1951), p.125

[48] W. Innes, "Letter V" <u>Reasons for Separating from The Church of Scotland</u> (Dundee, 1804), p.76

[49] W. Innes, "Letter VI" (ibid.), p.92

obedience to their commands, though they cannot convince the party that 'these' are right, my simple question is, On what authority is this claim founded?"[50]

We have seen above Innes' arguments for the unscriptural basis for Presbyterianism. The fundamental problem he has, however, is that it goes against what he sees as one of the first principles of being a Christian; that 'one must be persuaded in one's own mind'. Innes believed that personal enquiry into one's own Christianity should be seen as a duty. He wished every Christian to examine his religion for himself: "It would be too little to say he is entitled to do so: he is bound to do it, as every question relating to the revealed will of God has an undoubted claim to the attention of every individual."[51] Innes disagreed with the Rev. James Smith of Dundee that the majority of 'private Christians' were part of an 'untaught multitude', unable to interpret the word of God for themselves. Rather he argued that, while they may not be classical scholars who had read theology, the majority of Christians were "*taught in the world*, (the most valuable surely of all teaching)."[52] Thus, there was no argument to be made against individuals engaging with scripture in the context of their own lives and presenting what the will of God could reasonably be judged, in their opinion, to be.

In his works spanning fifty years Innes consistently held to this necessity, reiterating on several occasions that, "No human authority whatever can justify a man in complying with a requisition which he is convinced is inconsistent with the will of God."[53] Scottish Congregationalism was, says James Ross, "from the first of native growth, in the sense that its principles were adopted of necessity and spontaneously in order to give effect to the spiritual convictions and aspirations of men who had been spiritually quickened, and to whom spirituality and freedom of church-life and activity had become a necessity."[54] Congregational government was set out by Robert Haldane as being "exercised in the presence of the church itself, by its pastor and office-bearers, and with the consent of the members, independent of any other jurisdiction,"[55] allowing all members the right to question any aspect of Christian dogma or practice.

This was consistent with the Congregationalists' understanding of what 'the church' was. Rowland Hill said of the Kirk: "One would suppose according to them, *the church* existed not but under their establishment. Another church claims the same elusive character – the Church of Rome...But she should remember also, that the church, in a richer sense of the word, is a company of holy people, collected in the name of the Lord Jesus, though in an upper room, or

[50] W. Innes, The Power of the Presbyteries (Edinburgh, 1832), p.11-12
[51] W. Innes, Animadversions on a Late Pamphlet (Dundee, 1806), p. 21
[52] W. Innes, (ibid.), p,3
[53] W. Innes, "Letter V" Reasons for Separating from The Church of Scotland (Dundee, 1804), p.68
[54] J. Ross, A History of Congregational Independency in Scotland (Glasgow, 1900), p.77
[55] A. Haldane, The Lives of Robert Haldane of Airthrey, and of his Brother, James Alexander (London, 1853), p.219

in a private house...and the church still, though not established by law."[56] Moreover, for the Congregationalists, each person within every company of God's people as they envisaged it, was called to take up the challenge of *being* the church. Thus, wrote Innes, "We are surely not at liberty to tamper with the express rule of scripture and say, the business which our Lord committed to the general body, we will allow to be managed by a few individuals, while that body is never consulted."[57]

In the established church this liberty was not found. Even before ministers were ordained, the majority of their appointments were subject to patronage and, although this system had served three generations of his family, Innes joined the long debate over patronage, criticising it severely.

In 1804 he wrote, "Nothing can be more obvious from the whole spirit of Christianity, than that the relation between a pastor and his flock must be a voluntary one. The idea of such a relation, where the pastor is not the object of the people's choice, is an absurdity. Such a system may be carried on where a profession of religion is merely used as a political engine, or where the people are buried in gross ignorance or stupid indifference."[58]

Innes knew from his own experience that if a man had good representation then his ordination was a foregone conclusion. He criticised the law of patronage as one which denied the choice of the people; in the majority of parishes, ministers were ensconced because of the 'presentation' they had carried. As so many of those within the established church had relied on patronage to secure their positions it was not surprising to Innes that few should criticise the system. To do so himself, Innes had left the Church of Scotland and not all would be in a position to take that step – personally or financially – or would have the courage to do so.

Further, there were many who had no desire to call for reform: "The man ... who considers religion chiefly in the light of a useful political institution; as a valuable means of keeping the multitude in habits of decency and sobriety ... Such a man may well be supposed to consider the call of the people as quite unnecessary. It is not essential to his system."[59] For this reason, Innes foresaw little hope of reform on the issue.

Indeed, almost fifty years later, the same subject concerned him: "It is of special importance that the most perfect mutual confidence should subsist between a pastor and his flock."[60] If this was not the case then the challenge of individual responsibility for one's Christianity could not, for Innes, be met. "Each party should endeavour to discover his own duty from the word of God."[61] Only

---

[56] R. Hill, "A Series of Letters Occasioned by the Late Pastoral Admonition of the Church of Scotland…" (Edinburgh, 1799), p.21
[57] W. Innes, "Letter VI" <u>Reasons for Separating from The Church of Scotland</u> (Dundee, 1804), p,94
[58] W. Innes, "Letter V" (ibid.), p.62
[59] W. Innes, "Letter V" <u>Reasons for Separating from The Church of Scotland</u> (Dundee, 1804), p.74
[60] W. Innes, <u>Hints on Church Government</u> (Edinburgh, 1852), p.43
[61] W. Innes, (ibid.)

then could the ideal relation between a leader and his congregation foster mutual education and discovery. Hence Innes' view that patronage be out of the question. "It may institute a preaching station," he wrote, "but it cannot form a church....It is like a marriage... when it becomes a question how far the husband is entitled to exercise his authority, and how far the wife is bound to obey, the spirit of the relation is gone."[62]

There was no dissolution of the relation between Innes and the congregation of the Dundee Tabernacle where he remained minister for eight years. His leaving that church was the result of a shift in the theological beliefs of the Haldanes and the consequences these changes held in determining the way in which their churches were run.

In the early years of the nineteenth century James Alexander Haldane began to question the validity of infant baptism and by the end of 1804 he was determined to consider the subject in earnest. After four years, his studies convinced him that the only baptism with a scriptural basis was that of Believers' Baptism and in March 1808 he was himself baptised by immersion on the profession of his faith.[63] Within a year, Robert Haldane had reached the same theological conclusion as his brother. The results of their change of heart were far reaching for the churches they had founded. Robert Haldane felt it necessary to withdraw the level of funding he had previously given to the Tabernacles while infant baptism remained a fundamental part of their constitution. William Innes' stipend at Dundee had nevertheless been guaranteed, but his conscience led him to believe he could not accept the fee from someone who differed theologically; this despite now having a family of four children to support.

In Edinburgh the reaction to J.A. Haldane's conversion was varied and left the congregation of the Tabernacle so at odds that a split was inevitable between them. It had not been the intention of Haldane for the division to happen. His hopes were that despite his being unwilling to administer infant baptism, the congregation would allow him to remain as pastor while the sacrament could be administered by a colleague. Haldane said, "If we are all acting on conviction and both desiring to know the will of Jesus in this, and in all other respects, I have no apprehension of disunion. Of one thing I am sure, that all who love the Lord Jesus should, so far as they are agreed, walk by the same rule, and mind the same things..."[64] But this ideal of forbearance was not realised and the congregation haemorrhaged.

In 1809, having recently left his post at Dundee, William Innes agreed his move to Edinburgh in order that he might accept a call from around one hundred seceders of the Tabernacle to become their pastor. Together they formed a new Congregational Church which met in Bernard's Rooms, West Thistle Street. It was to be an appointment which lasted for only one year.

[62] W. Innes, (ibid.), p.44
[63] G. Yuille, History of the Baptists in Scotland (Glasgow, 1926), p58
[64] Cited: G. Escott, A History of Scottish Congregationalism (Glasgow, 1960), p.84

CHAPTER V
ENQUIRING TO BELIEVE

"When a man is content with his own conscience
he does not care to shine with the light of another's"

BERNARD OF CLAIRVAUX

That every aspect of Christian faith and doctrine should be open to question and enquiry was fundamental for William Innes. His was an enquiring mind by nature. From his time in Stirling, it is variously recorded that he would frequently meet his contemporaries for debate. Through his preaching and his day-to-day discussions with his various congregations and through the publication of several pamphlets and series of letters, he would share with the wider public the development of his thought.

Innes' fundamental principle that every Christian must be convinced of the beliefs they hold to and the confessions they make not only resulted in his own mind being restless but also made him curious as to the workings of the minds of those with whom he was acquainted. He wished to engage with those whom he witnessed as intelligently grappling with new ideas on theology and practice within the church; he wanted to be a part of their learning process and for their views to draw from him the clearest reasoning for his own systems of thought. Innes saw Christianity as a religion for all times; not in the sense that there was one answer which was to satisfy every generation. Rather, he saw that the Gospel is for every generation who must, themselves, understand in what way this is the case. "The religion of Christ," he writes, "is a combination of new principles with new practice. New principles are introduced into the mind, and these, when really embraced, must lead to new practice... No profession of the principles is of any avail, unless the practices follow; and on the other hand, no correctness of outward conduct can be well-pleasing to God, which does not flow from a belief of the truth, or those new principles which are revealed and enjoined as the spring of all holy obedience."[65]   The church, then, was for Innes a constantly evolving body of people whose responsibility it is to define itself in every time and place.

When the two Haldane brothers came independently to the conclusion that believers' baptism was the only form of the sacrament to have a scriptural basis, the implications for the Tabernacle churches across Scotland was sizeable. The congregation of the Edinburgh Tabernacle now divided into various groups whose new constitutions re-defined the principles which bound them together. It was to one such section of these Seceders that William Innes would spend eleven months ministering.

---

[65] Innes <u>Origin and Permanence of Christian Joy</u> (Edinburgh, 1828) p.32-33

In his own way, Innes appears to have relished the personal and spiritual challenges the Haldane's views necessitated; their new 'principles and practices' inadvertently changing the course his own life and spiritual development would take. For some time, Innes could find no reason to follow their lead and abandon his position, believing infant baptism to be in accordance with the will of God. But the line of enquiry was now uppermost in his mind.

Innes' writing on the subject of baptism is largely confined to his pamphlet Reflections of an Enquirer on the Subject of Baptism published more than thirty years after he first began examining his beliefs on the subject. As his decision to leave the Church of Scotland had not been an easy one, so, too, he initially felt ill at ease questioning the doctrine of baptism as set out by his forefathers – a doctrine to which he had submitted all his days:

> You have heard that I have changed my views on baptism. It is true, I have. All my prejudices I can assure you were in favour of my former sentiments, but I felt myself constrained to change my opinions, by what appeared to me at least satisfactory evidence and to avow that change… It was painful to differ from many esteemed Christian friends who still maintain this doctrine. I felt the difficulty…of acknowledging, after having often argued in its defence, that I was mistaken. [66]

Sixteen years after his ordination, Innes' circumstances prompted hesitations on a subject which his conscience directed him to discuss with friends. Innes conversed with men of both persuasions, objectively considering the arguments they had to offer while revisiting passages from scripture himself.

Innes had always been convinced by the argument for infant baptism based on the Abrahamic covenant which likens baptism with circumcision as corresponding 'seals of the righteousness of faith' of the Old and New testaments; thus, baptism should be administered to the children of believers in the same way as, on the eighth day, circumcision was given to Abraham's children. While seeming plausible on the surface, on examination, Innes came to reject this theory. To accept the parallel requires one to interpret the 'seal of the righteousness of faith' of circumcision as a confirmation to each person of "a personal interest in some blessings temporal or spiritual."[67] But Innes contends that, in the first place, it is not easy to discern either what is sealed, or indeed, that something was sealed to all those who received it. Circumcision was commanded to be received by all the servants in Abraham's family and to their children also, as well as all male children and slaves of any stranger if it was their wish to partake in the Pesach meal. However, that all who were commanded to receive the ordinance should have been interested in some temporal good, Innes sees as having been disproved; "the proselytes and their slaves had no interest in

---

[66] W. Innes, Reflections of an Enquirer on the Subject of Baptism (Edinburgh, 1840), p.3 / p.22
[67] W. Innes, (ibid.), p.3

Canaan."[68] "And no one," Innes argues, "will allege it sealed spiritual blessings to every one to whom it was applied, as many of those commanded to receive it had no interest in such blessings."[69] Circumcision, thus, sealed no blessings on those who were required to submit to it by Divine appointment.

In addition to this, Innes saw fault with the understanding that circumcision could confer righteousness on a person through his consideration of the story of Ishmael who, as one of Abraham's family was required to be circumcised (Gen.xvii.21). Here, while Ishmael is to receive temporal blessings, yet the covenant is to be established with his son Isaac. Thus, "It could not be viewed then as sealing, or confirming, any thing to Ishmael as an individual, while he was, by express revelation, excluded from that very covenant, of which it was the sign."[70]

On Innes' understanding the 'seal of righteousness of faith' was to be understood as "a seal or a standing memorial of the fact that Abraham's faith was imputed to him for righteousness, and thus the doctrine that whosoever hath the same faith, it shall be imputed to him in like manner."[71] On this reading, the sign was equally efficacious whether it was conferred upon an infant, a slave or an adult Jew. Innes goes on to say that this interpretation is backed up by the Apostle Paul's reasoning on the subject in his Letter to the Romans (iv.11), where he shows that faith was sufficient without circumcision as Abraham was justified before the event.

Innes states, "Here then is the essential difference between circumcision and baptism. The former was no indication of a personal interest in spiritual blessings. It could not be so, if the enjoyment of spiritual blessings is connected with spirituality of mind, because it was commanded, on pain of death, to be observed by the whole nation, even in their most degenerate times. Baptism," he continues, "being connected with a profession of faith, is an expression of a personal interest in the blessings of the new covenant."[72]

One can see from scripture, Innes argues, the requirement of this 'personal interest' necessary for Christian baptism. The Ethiopian eunuch is told he must believe with all his heart before the baptism is conferred. Christians who are baptised have 'put on Christ'. "But how can men put on Christ but by a public confession of faith in Him?"[73] asks Innes. Further, it is individuals, as opposed to nations or families or whole peoples, who are called to be disciples of Christ and it is only through professing to be a disciple of Christ that one can be declared a Christian. Thus, Innes could draw the conclusion that "one was the religion of *birth*, the other a religion of *conviction*; the one comes by blood; of the other it is expressly said, 'to be not of blood, nor of the will of the flesh, nor of the will of

---

[68] W. Innes, (ibid.), p.4
[69] W. Innes, Reflections of an Enquirer on the Subject of Baptism (Edinburgh, 1840), p.4
[70] W. Innes, (ibid.)
[71] W. Innes, (ibid.), p.5
[72] W. Innes, (ibid), p.5-6
[73] W. Innes, (ibid.), p.6

man, but of God,' John.i.13;"[74] Christianity, a religion of conviction required faith and obedience, something which infants could not be expected to possess.

The issue of infant baptism led Innes naturally into a further criticism of the polity of the church he had served for nearly two decades of his professional life. Being a national institution, the Church of Scotland could be seen to subscribe to infant baptism as a means of securing its position of authority, through gaining an ensured membership and thus maintaining its powerful dominance in society. If there were only the established national churches then all children born to Christian parents would be as much members of that church as they were subjects of the government. Hence, the practice of infant baptism as adopted by the institutional church could be condemned on account of its "deceiving men by recognizing them as Christians by birth, while they have no claim to the character."[75] In light of this, Innes said, "I cannot see how the purity and spiritual nature of Christ's kingdom can be maintained along with it." The true church of Christ as he now saw it was a gathering of those who professed their faith in Jesus and all that he taught.

The spread of new ideas through the church may have provoked "contention, strife of words and divisions"[76] but for Innes there was no alternative. In 1810, he became a Baptist. His decision was not an unconsidered 'jumping on the bandwagon'; it was a conscientious decision which was ultimately taken regardless of the theological choices made by his contemporaries. Innes was 'convinced in his own mind': "When my attention from particular circumstances was called to the subject," he said, "I neither DARED to decline to examine it more fully, nor to disregard the convictions thus produced."[77] Innes had set himself the same standards as all men. He wrote, "I cannot conceive of how any man can maintain a conscience void of offence to God, who can either deliberately neglect such examination or fail to act on its result." Circumstances led him to examine baptism and it was the consequences of his adopting Baptist principles which were to determine a change, once more, in his pastoral duties.

Having taken over the ministry of the Congregational Church meeting in Bernard's Rooms who had formed themselves expressly because of their support for the doctrine of infant baptism, Innes had to inform them personally and directly of his change of heart, and resigned from the pastorate at the request of the majority of those gathered. However, Innes had supporters for the sincerity and honesty of his position and seventeen of those men and women were to continue to be led in worship by him.

---

[74] W. Innes, (ibid.), p.9
[75] W. Innes, Reflections of an Enquirer on the Subject of Baptism (Edinburgh, 1840), p.10
[76] W. D Mc Naughton "A Few Historical Notes on Scottish Congregationalism" http://www.westendcongregationalchurch.org/congregation.htm, p.6
[77] W. Innes, (ibid.), p.22

Encouraged by this small group, William Innes founded a Baptist church in the same year of 1810 which, for the first three years of its meeting, would gather at Laing's Academy on East Thistle Street, Edinburgh. Innes explained his position to those who gathered round him:

> While I have ever been disposed to regard, with the most sincere affection and esteem many Christian brethren who differ from me on this point – while I feel that I have much to learn from many of them, both in point of knowledge, Christian zeal, and personal piety, and while I cordially rejoice in the success of every minister of Christ, by whatever name he is called, yet all must allow that the conclusion to which any one is led after the most careful examination of the subject, is that which must point out the path of duty to *him*. It is only by acting according to his conviction that any man can...move towards God and towards man. Though I had always entertained the same views of Christian forbearance I now do, the church with which I was connected viewed the subject differently[78]

It was the liberality of the minds of that small number who joined Innes Sunday by Sunday which allowed the new church to be unique for its time from its conception, being founded on the principles of open communion and open membership.

Innes had viewed the issue of baptism from both sides and although convinced in his own mind of the scriptural precedent for believers' baptism, he, like Robert Haldane before him, did not wish his convictions to result in disunion from those who could find justification for themselves that infant baptism was the will of God. "Evidence certainly strikes different minds very differently, and on this principle," Innes said, "I can exercise the most unlimited forbearance to those who, having conscientiously examined the subject, can say that they hold infant baptism to be scriptural."[79] So it was, that of the seventeen who made up the first congregation under Innes' ministry, independent of any movement, only some of them had reached the same conclusion as their leader on the subject of baptism. The rest regarded it of paramount importance that the discrepancy in their opinions should not mean they should not have fellowship with those whom they loved as 'brothers'.

The church in East Thistle Street offered membership to any person who professed to love Jesus Christ as their Lord and Saviour. Although the proviso was made that whoever was to lead the ministry of the congregation should be a Baptist, no one who had not been baptised as a believer would be excluded from full membership of the congregation. The policy of open membership was logically accompanied by the policy of open communion which was also practiced

---

[78] Cited: A. Baines, <u>History of Dublin Street Baptist Church, Edinburgh 1885-1958</u> (Edinburgh, 1958) p. 24
[79] W. Innes, <u>Reflections of an Enquirer on the Subject of Baptism</u> (Edinburgh, 1840), p.22

by these pioneering Christians.[80] The Lord's Table was therefore open to all who made that same profession of faith in Christ; baptism was not to determine who should eat the bread or drink the wine. Each member of that congregation accepted and found truth in Innes' belief that,

> In baptism...the spiritual is placed above the ritual, and though it is the duty of everyone to inquire into all the will of God, and so far as he knows to obey it, I feel that I should be reversing this order, that I should be sacrificing the *spirit* to the *letter* if I rejected from Christian communion, one who gave evidence which I could not question...that Christ had received him, merely because he differed from me regarding the observance of a particular ordinance.[81]

In 1845 he wrote to a friend how open communion had been a principle he had long since admired. "I understand by it," he wrote, "holding communion with those whom we believe to be Christians, in things which we are agreed, without any compromise of principle in things which we differ."[82] For Innes this mutual forbearance was essential to the Christian church and had at last found a spiritual home where the Christian virtue of tolerance was put into practice. "The Church is not OURS. It is the Lord's. The Table is not OURS. It is the Lord's", as a contemporary statement of that congregation still declares.

The subject of mutual forbearance and its implications for Christian Union were to inform the polity of that young church and the majority of Innes' subsequent writing.

---

[80] "It is the earliest of our churches based on Open principles" G. Yuille, History of the Baptists in Scotland (Glasgow, 1926), p.62

[81] W. Innes, Open Communion and Christian Forbearance (Edinburgh, 1845), p.8

[82] W. Innes, Open Communion and Christian Forbearance (Edinburgh, 1845), p.4-5

CHAPTER VI

IN THE NAME OF THE FATHER

"Tout comprende rend trés indulgent"
"To know all makes one tolerant"
MME DE STAËL

In 1813, the numbers of people gathering to hear William Innes conduct worship had grown so as to necessitate a move to a larger, purpose-built chapel on Elder Street at the East End of Edinburgh's New Town. Elder Street Baptist Church did not gather folk on the scale of the Tabernacles, but one senses that the principles on which it was founded would not have lent themselves to such numbers where those attending could remain completely anonymous. It was desired of all members that they should watch and care for one another; co-joined into one body, their mutual usefulness served to edify the whole. This, thought Innes, was "the foundation of all gospel unity among believers."[83]

The realisation of this model of the church impressed Dr. W. Lindsay Alexander who described Elder Street Church as,

> A small and somewhat select community, containing among its members and office-bearers some very choice specimens of the Christian, and some rather remarkable developments of individual character. A lively state of religious feeling prevailed, and much friendly intercourse took place amongst the members, and all were bound by common ties of spiritual interest and fraternal regard.[84]

Innes had instilled in the community the sense that their common bond as Christian disciples was sufficiently strong as to allow for variances of opinion on matters of doctrine. These variances, he held, were unavoidable, Christianity being a spiritual religion of the mind and human minds belonging to so many individuals as to make total agreement on all matters impossible.

Not only human minds, but human lives – the circumstances people find themselves in, the upbringings they receive – provide every individual with different systems of reference from which to draw these conclusions. Thus, Innes asserts: "When we take into view the effect of early prejudice, of early habits and associations, we need not wonder that there should be a difference of opinion on minor matters among the real disciples of Christ. But what we maintain is that this should not prevent them from feeling themselves united in the great fundamental truths and, on every suitable occasion, being prepared to express

---

[83] W. Innes, <u>Open Communion and Christian Forbearance</u> (Edinburgh, 1845), p.14
[84] Cited: A. Baines, <u>History of Dublin Street Baptist Church, Edinburgh 1858-1958</u> (Edinburgh, 1958), p.8

this union"[85]. In such cases where disagreement on doctrine and practice arose, Innes believed it necessary only to "resort to human prudence in the application of the rules already laid down"[86]. This he saw as the responsibility of all gatherings of Christ's disciples to allow the message of the Gospel to speak to them.

"Faith and love," wrote Innes, "are spoken of as the two graces which distinguish Christians from the rest of the world, and mark their union among themselves."[87]   It was thus through and in the spirit of faith and love that he called his friends to recognize forbearance as essential to living according to the will of God. Too often, he had seen Christian communities torn apart by the fact that the spirit of the Gospel had been forsaken at the expense of the letter of the law.

This criticism was not merely directed to the established church. Forbearance was not an habitual custom of the independent churches in Scotland! Many independents were narrower or more conservative than the Moderate-dominated Kirk. Followers of the teachings of, for example, John Glas (1695-1773) and Robert Sandeman (1718-1771) were against the principles of mutual tolerance, the consequences of which – having a body of people gathered who did not agree on all matters of faith and practice – did not align with their understanding of church unity.

Innes' message was equally directed to the majority of Baptist churches in contemporary Scotland.   An Account of the Faith and Practices of the Scotch Baptists picks up on a passage of scripture cited as a precedent for Christian tolerance to convey a clear line to the members of their union running contrary to the views of the congregation at Elder Street:

> The mutual forbearance enjoined, Rom. xiv, relates only to the Jewish distribution about meats and days; but was never intended to make any one Christian doctrine or duty indifferent or a matter of forbearance. 'Christ's religion contains no *non essentials*, which his people may observe if they please, or may neglect, without displeasing him.' His authority can never clash with itself, by giving laws, and at the same time a dispensation to neglect them. We consider it our duty to be all of *one mind* in everything that regards our *faith* and *practice*.[88]

This is not to say that Innes or the fellow members of the Elder Street congregation believed any doctrine should be dispensed with. Indeed, Innes agrees with the fact that the regulations practised by the Apostles and the churches they planted are "clearly quoted as binding, and sufficient to settle

[85] W. Innes, Open Communion and Christian Forbearance (Edinburgh, 1845), p.5-6
[86] W. Innes, "Letter II" Reasons for Separating from The Church of Scotland (Dundee, 1804), p.21
[87] W. Innes, (ibid.), p.4
[88] G. Jamieson, An Account of the Faith and Practices of the Scotch Baptists (Paisley, 1829), p.32

disputes,"[89] yet, he says, "When they come to particulars, there will probably be a considerable diversity of opinion respecting what some of these regulations really are, as well as the degree of precision with which they are revealed."[90]

Innes believed that knowledge of revealed truth could always be improved upon; that "it is impossible to conceive in what a variety of ways the great Head of the church may direct the attention of his people to more enlarged views of divine truth."[91] Because the Church and the world in which it is are continually thrown into new situations it cannot be so that God would require it a duty to be 'all of *one mind* in everything that regards our *faith* and *practice*'. Thus, *his* disagreement with the orthodox Baptist position of the early nineteenth century expressed above was the same as he had with the teachings of several of the independent branches of the church; *his* disagreement was about the nature of church unity.

By the time Elder Street was more than twenty years established, however, the Scotch Baptist Churches were addressed and it was the view Innes had long held – as to the necessity of Christian tolerance for there to be true unity of the church – which was promoted.

True unity was not seen as a unity of sentiment (although such unity was not rejected on its own merits[92]) rather, it was seen as a unity of spirit. "Mutual forbearance is essential to the maintenance of the fervent love and peaceful affection which ought to distinguish the disciples of Christ. It is impossible without it, to maintain that unity of spirit which ought to pervade a Church." Diversity of sentiment was seen to be an unavoidable bi-product of the human condition, therefore forbearance was seen to be fundamental if the church was to unite in the spirit of faith and love. Innes said, "If a gathering of Christians meets with the knowledge that forbearance will be exercised this, in turn, promotes a spirit of free enquiry enabled by "mutual confidence, which is essential to Christian fellowship."[93]

The problem with the unity of sentiment is spelt out in an exhortation addressed to the Baptist churches in 1834. The author points out that, "Wherever uniformity of sentiment exists, if that can be supposed possible, forbearance may be discarded as a useless virtue, of which the Christian has no experience, and need never exercise."[94] He goes on to point out that the Apostle Paul was not of the opinion that shared sentiment was the basis of church unity: "On the contrary, he considered forbearance as the virtue by which the union of believers was to be maintained."[95] In Ephesus, his object was to build up one family in Christ of reconciled Jew and Gentile converts. Christ taught of charity and liberality of

---

[89] W. Innes, "Letter II" <u>Reasons for Separating from The Church of Scotland</u> (Dundee, 1804), p.18
[90] W. Innes, (ibid.), p.19
[91] W. Innes, "Letter II" <u>Reasons for Separating from The Church of Scotland</u> (Dundee, 1804), p.22
[92] see: W. Innes, <u>Remarks on Christian Union</u> (Edinburgh, 1811), p.2ff.
[93] W. Innes, (ibid.). p.10
[94] -----, <u>An Exhortation to Christian Forbearance and Union</u> (Edinburgh, 1834) p.4
[95] -----, (ibid.), p.4

sentiment, of love and faith rather than of dogmas and rigid laws. Innes and the author of the above exhortation, whose name is unpublished, saw this in their readings of the Gospel.

From the writing of the New Testament, further illustration is given for the scriptural authority of forbearance as essential to the unity of the church. Previous to the first years of Christianity, the Jews had worshipped one God and were separated from associating with Gentile Nations. Meanwhile, among the Gentile communities there was worship and adoration of several deities. Christian disciples, however, are "taken from every nation, and kindred, and people, and tongue,"[96] yet all are one in Christ.

It was also interestingly observed by this independent voice that:

> It was not till Christianity came to be established by law, that forbearance was discarded – that unity of sentiment was required – that, for this purpose, creeds and formal confessions of faith were framed – that liturgies were adopted,- that divisions took place and multiplied...That, notwithstanding the diversity of country, and manners, and customs, which distinguished and characterized the first Christians, and the differences of sentiment which are known to have existed in the primitive Churches, and which we, in the present day, would consider fatal to union, it was not till the third century that dissent or separation among Christians took place; and then the separation arose, not so much on account of differences of opinion as to religious observances and ordinances.[97]

Thus, for more than two centuries, the church can be seen as deviating little from embodying the spirit of the Gospel through its recognition and valuing of the virtue of forbearance. It was to this model of church that Innes and others wished to return.

The church at Elder Street, however, stood out amongst its contemporary Baptist congregations in actually achieving this position. Where many churches had split over the disagreement of the sacrament of baptism – a matter which was close to Innes following the failure of the Tabernacle churches to remain united – the congregation was constituted *around* the fact that the matter need not be agreed upon. The members settled that it was enough to say the same spirit moved each one of them to understand baptism as they did; that they had all made a common profession of their faith; that trust in this and in the love of Jesus Christ was the prerequisite for their bond of fellowship. No doubt they would have put their names to such a declaration as was made as a plea for 'true' union:

> But we should never forget, that the ordinances of religion, and our association as brethren are but the means of promoting our edification,

---

[96] -----, (ibid.), p.6
[97] -----, (ibid,), pp.5-.6

and of building us up in our most holy faith; and that however important they are for these purposes, it is faith in Christ, and love to God, and to our brethren, which are the essentials of religion.[98]

While still a member of the Church of Scotland, Innes had been disturbed by the lack of tolerance in presbytery meetings and at the General Assembly, standing once to ask of his contemporaries, "Are not these men you sit with in church courts, in one sense, still your brethren?"[99]; his desire had long since been to place Christianity, as he saw it, above 'churchianity'.

In 1810, Innes foresaw criticism of the adoption of the principles of open membership and open communion at Elder Street and struggled to convince many of his friends that he had no hesitation in joining in communion with a Paedobaptist church (as he had no hesitation in joining with an Episcopalian or Presbyterian or Independent) because he saw no supposition that this should require him to relinquish his own principles. "The difference is known and recognised in both sides," he said, "But I unite with my brethren in...Christ. In so far as we have thus attained, we walk by the same rule – mind the same things – and I am happy to unite with them in celebrating the event which forms the grand bond of union in the world of glory."[100]

Innes recognized the objection of some Baptists to the fact that Elder Street's policy of open membership led to open communion. As the majority of Baptist churches saw it at the time, only those baptized were received into the first churches and as infant baptism was not, in their opinion, 'true baptism', they found they could not accept communion with those who had not made a public confession of faith. Innes respected this position and retaliated only by saying that for him and for his followers, such matters did not concern them unduly. Of his Paedobaptist brethren, Innes suggested all that could be said was that, in the opinion of Baptists, "they mistake the proper way of observing this ordinance."[101] He adds to this a quotation from John Bunyan: "Though a Christian community mistakes the proper application of an ordinance...this does not destroy their character as a church of Christ,"[102] along with pointing to the fact that though the Israelites did not practise circumcision for forty years, yet they were still considered 'the church of God'. Thus, for Innes, the rejection of Paedobaptists as unworthy partakers of communion could not be countenanced.[103] "The truth is," he said, "that where any one is interested in this foundation of all gospel unity, he may demand communion with any church in the world, and ought not to be

[98] -----, _An Exhortation to Christian Forbearance and Union_ (Edinburgh, 1834), p.7

[99] W. Innes, "Letter VI" _Reasons for Separating from The Church of Scotland_ (Dundee, 1804), p.85

[100] W. Innes, _Open Communion and Christian Forbearance_ (Edinburgh, 1845), p.7

[101] W.Innes, (ibid.), p.8

[102] cited: W.Innes, (ibid.), p.16

[103] Cf. W.Innes, _Remarks on Christian Union_ (Edinburgh, 1811), p.15ff.

refused..."[104] Christian forbearance was, thus, of the most fundamental importance.

The virtues of humility, meekness, love and charity which were deemed necessary for forbearance to be practised, were, to an extent, also necessary for Elder Street Chapel as they sought to be inclusive to all Christian perspectives in their approach to preaching and learning, as well as around the Lord's Table. Innes had written shortly before the congregation were to move to their new home, that, "I am sorry to think (this) can only be said by so few, that my pulpit is open to the ministers of Christ of whatever denomination, who may occasionally visit this part of the country and feel themselves at liberty to occupy it."[105] The fact that in the following decades there was no shift to emulate this practice elsewhere, concerned Innes. He wrote in 1845, "I can never consider...our union what it ought to be, and such as it is likely to attain this most desirable consummation, till every minister of the Gospel shall be able, without let or surmise, to invite to his pulpit any other minister who would preach the same truth."[106] Innes was genuine in his desire that the Christian religion should be presented in all its fullness and that, only then, could the glory of God be seen to be proclaimed.

No doubt, his views were partly tempered by his early experiences in the Church of Scotland. It was once asserted that Innes and his friend and relation Greville Ewing were said to be "less fettered in the performance of their duty prior to their separation than they are since, when every member of the churches in which they preside, possesses authority to judge and decide on any part of their ministerial conduct,"[107] but this was firmly denied. Congregational principles, the freedom of enquiry, the breadth and depth of preaching possible through the invitation to those of varying denominations and persuasions to share their knowledge of the divine truth, provided Innes, at least, with a freer and more true expression of his Christianity than he had ever known before.

While pioneering liberal theology and practice at Elder Street Chapel, William Innes was also testing the liberality of his wife and children for whom the financial strain of his acceptance to move to Edinburgh had been testing. While Innes was minister to the Tabernacle at Dundee his stipend had been assured at a rate of £200 per annum. This level of support had been maintained by the congregation of Tabernacle Seceders at Bernard's Rooms. However, on his removal to Laing's Academy, the congregation had struggled to produce enough funds to pay him the sum of only £100 per annum for the first decade at least.

From the position of near destitution, Innes decided some years into his time at Elder Street to invest what little capital he did have into a publishing and bookselling company. Much of his own material found its way into distribution

---

[104] W. Innes, (ibid.), p.30
[105] W. Innes, Letter to the Editor of the *Christian Instructor* (Edinburgh, 1812), p.30
[106] W. Innes, Open Communion and Christian Forbearance (Edinburgh, 1845), p.29
[107] Rev. James Smith, cited: W. Innes, Animadversions on a Late Pamphlet (Dundee, 1806), p.7

through this scheme, as well as pamphlets from leading evangelists and several good American books which he deemed the British public should have access to. The venture was successful for some little while. However, as the material from other sources, bar his own pen, became harder to afford the rights to, the firm became insolvent and Innes lost his small wealth. His wife was never to learn of the eventual failure of his company, her death coming shortly before its closure.

Innes' eldest son, also William, followed his father into the bookselling trade while also leading Sunday evening classes at Elder Street. The journals of his wife, Martha, were published after her death in 1884 and recount some of her earliest memories of her father-in-law and of her time at Elder Street to which she came on her moving to Edinburgh in the summer of 1831.

Martha arrived in Edinburgh an Episcopalian but chose to worship at Elder Street. During her first twelve months in the city she inquired into the subject of baptism and after much conversation with her pastor and friends she chose to submit to the ordinance. She notes in her journal the desire to rise to the challenge made real within that congregation; asking in prayer, "fit me for discharging the duties that rest upon each member to another; and bless me with a spiritual union in heart with all, that we may be helpers together of each other's faith, not sparring, but exhorting in faith, that Christ may be formed in us". Each member was required to edify others in their everyday life and this appealed to Martha's sense of Christian duty. After her marriage four years later, she became more involved in the worship of the church, leading prayer on several occasions.

It is in the journals of Martha Innes that we learn of a time when forbearance was a virtue which the congregation at large found difficult to hold to, despite the support of their pastor's ideals. In an entry for February 19th, 1840, Martha wrote, "My mind is much exercised about the concerns of the Church in Elder Street. I fear the spirit opposed to that of Christ already works...What has given rise to this unhappy feeling, I regret is in the choice of a joint pastor with Mr. Innes."[108] After the loss of his wife and his business, Innes had become weaker in health and at the suggestion of the congregation he agreed it would be best to share the work of pastoral visitation and preaching with another like-minded person. The problem came when Innes recommended a Mr. Cameron for the charge. Mr. Cameron was not a Baptist, and the constitution of Elder Street stipulated that, while the members need not subscribe to Baptist principles, the minister must. Mr. Cameron had been a popular visiting preacher but the prospect of his becoming a permanent pastor upset the majority. It seemed that the liberality on which the congregation prided itself had its limits after all.

Martha Innes was keen that the congregation should welcome Mr. Cameron for his fine teaching and "the effects of his preaching". Her words could have belonged to Dr. Innes himself:

---

[108] W. Innes Jr. Ed., Memoir of Martha Innes (London, 1844), p.143

It is necessary to take care that we do not lay undue stress upon any one part of the divine word, and especially when that part is merely an outward expression of love to the saviour – for it is much easier to demonstrate our profession by the sacrifices which people ordinarily make to follow out the principles of adult baptism than to walk daily, hourly, as we are enjoined to do with God.[109]

Despite her wishes, however, a meeting of the congregation rejected the proposal to call Mr. Cameron and it was left several months until Mr. Innes' second proposal to the church, Mr. Jonathan Watson of Cupar, was quickly approved. It was the view of Martha Innes at least, that as the troubles amongst the congregation had subsided, something of the previous temperament had settled, the congregation realising that its growth occasioned an increase in the responsibility of each member to exhibit "a higher standard of Christian principle and practice than (had) hitherto (been) manifested."[110]

On August 30th, 1841, Martha Innes recorded that, "the church was crowded to excess."[111] It was her solemn wish that, as Mr. Innes continued to desire, every member should remember their personal accountability and not rest satisfied with their pastor's labour, "unless we digest it for the benefit of others and, as we receive light, reflect it."[112]

William Innes was to survive his wife for some nineteen years, his death being recorded on the 8th of March, 1855 in the sixty-second year of his professional ministry. He continued to preach until the end of his life, giving his time to the extended family of his congregation. While he prided himself on the ultimate security Elder Street had in the mutual confidence of its members to address issues as they wished, and to welcome as members and as partakers of communion all who confessed their faith, the fundamental happiness Innes found there is summed up by a sentence he penned shortly after its founding; a statement which he had desired to be true in all the walks of his life: that "We account it our greatest pleasure to live for one another."[113]

---

[109] W. Innes Jr. Ed., Memoir of Martha Innes (London, 1844), p.144
[110] W. Innes Jr. Ed., (ibid.), p.180
[111] W. Innes Jr. Ed., (ibid.), p.187
[112] W. Innes Jr. Ed., Memoir of Martha Innes (London, 1844), p.188
[113] W. Innes, Remarks on Christian Union (Edinburgh, 1811), p34

CONCLUSION

"Expect great things from God
Attempt great things for God"

WILLIAM CAREY

He was the very type of a true Scottish gentleman; slightly built, with a fine forehead and eyes full of kindness and tenderness. He dressed in the stately old-fashioned way with black silk stockings and knee-breeches, and even in old age he was very handsome. He had a singular power of attraction...[114]

His was the interpenetrating, binding charity – 'the bond of perfectness'...No man could pray with more sincerity...To be useful seems with him to have been the one aim of all he did...and nothing did he ensure success in this beneficent aim more than by the singular transparency of his moral character and the beautiful consistency of his Christian life.[115]

****

From his earliest years, growing up between the Scottish Borders and Edinburgh, William Innes' life was imbued with the influence of the church. His father, grandfather and those whom he tended to board with when he was at school instilled a sense of religious duty, but rather than accepting this unquestioningly, Innes' curious nature embraced these principles on his own terms. Having spent nine years studying theology, he was intent on probing his religion to enable him to address any point of doctrine and to allow him to converse at the deepest level with his friends and contemporaries.

Circumstance placed the ordained Church of Scotland minister in the parish of Stirling, while his charge including the chaplaincy to the Garrison in the Castle there put him in touch with the Haldane brothers. Their meeting and Innes' subsequent encouragement of their interest in mission and evangelising lit the touch paper for one of the most concerted and successful independent movements of its kind in Scottish church history.

Innes' conscience - his strong desire to do what was 'right' - deepened his tendency to enquire. He unquestionably felt a strong sense of loyalty to the established church, being frequently at pains to point out that when embarking

---

[114] Description recorded by the daughter of one of William Innes' deacons who remembered Innes herself from Elder Street days. (1893) Cited: A. Baines, History of Dublin Street Baptist Church, Edinburgh 1885-1958 (Edinburgh, 1958), p.25

[115] A.C. Thomas, Dr. Innes and his Times (Edinburgh, 1885), p.29

37

on areas of questioning, his prejudices were to find justification for the position his forefathers had held before him. It was his conscience, however, and his loyalty to the authority of God's will as he found it to be in scripture which was to determine his leaving the Church of Scotland and for the subsequent developments in his personal theology. The central tenets he felt compelled to relinquish were Presbyterianism and Infant Baptism.

Innes ultimately rejected Presbyterianism because of its hierarchical system of representation; the layers of unfounded authority subordinating the involvement of the true church – the congregation – in the running of affairs and in worship. Congregational polity appealed, on the other hand, because through their involvement in all church matters, each member was respected and this, in turn, was conducive to their improvement in knowledge and to their satisfaction.[116] Presbyterianism diminished personal conviction and for Innes was therefore directly opposed to the general spirit of the word of God as, he believed, "the moment that compulsion is introduced, spiritual worship is destroyed."[117]

Innes wished to encourage every person to take responsibility for living according to their convictions as he had done. He wished to promote the influence each person could make on others through the conduct of their daily lives. "Every one, however limited his sphere, tends to swell the tide of opinion,"[118] he wrote. "Say not that you have no talent...All have some. It does not need much talent or great knowledge, it needs only common sense and earnest piety."[119]

Unsurprisingly, the man who valued the response of each individual to their own calling to follow Christ could subscribe to the doctrine of infant baptism for a limited time. As an infant could not be persuaded in its own mind, the sacrament of Baptism could mean nothing to it. For Innes, Baptism was connected with self-examination of which an infant is not capable; ultimately, he said, "Baptism is in Scripture connected with believing."[120] Having come to this conclusion, Innes had no choice but change his life according to his conclusions.

This would have far reaching consequences, not only for himself but for his family also. It was well known to him that to live the Gospel out as faithfully to one's understanding as possible often came at some cost; genuine Christian living was not the easiest path. As Alexander Haldane notes, apart from his "ministerial faithfulness and amiable character," Innes made "great sacrifices for the sake of the Gospel."[121] Innes first gave up a comfortable parish position when he resigned his charge in Stirling, then took a substantial cut in his wages upon his

---

[116] See W. Innes, "Letter III" Reasons for Separating from The Church of Scotland (Dundee, 1804), pp.28-30
[117] W. Innes, "Letter IV" (ibid.), p.47
[118] W. Innes, "Letter VI" Reasons for Separating from The Church of Scotland (Dundee, 1804), p.89
[119] W. Innes, Responsibility; or Improve your Privileges (Edinburgh, 1843), p.65
[120] W. Innes, Letter to the Editor of the Christian Instructor (Edinburgh, 1812), p.14
[121] A. Haldane, The Lives of Robert Haldane of Airthrey, and of his Brother, James Alexander (London, 1853), p.369

leaving the Tabernacle church. Innes also wrote of a "coldness and reserve"[122] he experienced from some with whom he had once been a colleague, although many acquaintances admired his courage and faithfulness to the cause of living out his Christianity and remained friends and admirers throughout his lifetime. Those who did break their relations with him he felt sorry to lose but concluded that, "When this is put in competition with what (I am) convinced to be obedience to the will of Christ, there is no room to hesitate.[123]"

Indeed, Innes took many minds with him on his journey and constantly promoted the ideal that differences on particular theological points need not separate any Christians from one another. The spirit of faith and love and the ultimate desire to serve God together with mutual forbearance of one another should unite all Christians in all times and places. As the Rev. Alfred Thomas said after his death, Innes devoted his life "to the healing of strifes and divisions in the Church."[124]

He did so through encouragement and persuasion rather than by compelling his congregations to accept his views unquestioned. Innes worked slowly – taking months and sometimes years to draw firm conclusions on matters of importance – and he shared himself with others in the same way. Thomas' experience of Innes was that, "There was certainly nothing about him, mentally or morally, that reminded one of those detached meteors that shoot across the midnight sky, and then suddenly leaves the world in gloom; his was the happiness to resemble the soft, subduing light, which quietly but universally embraces the world. If he quietly dazzled less than some of his compeers, it was his province to please more than most of them."[125]

Innes was a quiet man and, by all accounts, a modest man, who accounted for the ever-increasing numbers of those who came to hear him preach, in Stirling, in Dundee, in Bernard's Rooms and in Elder Street Chapel, to the power of God rather than the force of his words. Innes was awarded an Honorary Doctor of Divinity degree from Washington College, Pennsylvania, in 1848. No record survives at the college as to why this should have been awarded to a Scottish Baptist minister but he received it nonetheless. We are told, however, that while he accepted it with pride he never paraded it.[126]

In summing up the life of William Innes, Thomas made some fine assessments of those things Innes had most wished to impart to those whom his life touched. Recounted here, they present a man whose life was, indeed, determined by both conscience and circumstance:

> This now completed life says to you...get principles of action... It says your spiritual prosperity and your usefulness depend on fidelity to your

---

[122] W. Innes, (ibid.), p.29
[123] W. Innes, Letter to the Editor of the *Christian Instructor* (Edinburgh, 1812), p.14
[124] A.C. Thomas, Dr. Innes and his Times (Edinburgh, 1885), p.16
[125] A.C. Thomas, (ibid.), p.28-9
[126] A.C. Thomas, Dr. Innes and his Times (Edinburgh, 1885), p23

convictions of truth and duty. It says that your solution of doubts respecting truth and duty mainly depends on your willingness to follow the truth at any cost... The life of Dr. Innes says...that to be right needs not so much great mental endowments, as strong moral determination *to do right* whenever it is found... This life says that none of us need to be passive under the influence of the great moral forces that are at work in our times... But the most beautiful lesson of this completed life is to the warring sects of the Church of Christ. Here is a life that proves with a singular power that the *love of truth* – the love of all God's truth in Christian doctrine – all God's truth in Christian institutions – may be blended with love for all God's people, however they may differ from us in creed.[127]

Innes' life was to be an example to those who followed him. Indeed, in the context of the congregation he founded his influence remains: worshipping as Dublin Street Baptist Church, when Elder Street became too small to house that particular family of God's people, and now as Canonmills Church, open membership and open communion are still bedrocks of the constitution. The pioneering spirit of the members of that church lives on too, as today they share in a Corporate Ministry.

The Corporate Ministry is one in which the whole congregation shares in the pastoral work of the church because they are *all* the Body of Christ, broken and re-membered every day; a community of "inextricably linked and interdependent parts of a WHOLE who exist for the nourishment of each other", as a contemporary statement of Canonmills Church reads, and who exist to share in the ongoing work of Jesus Christ in the world of our time.

It is an embodiment of the Church of which Innes surely would approve. Also, the fact that the congregation welcomes visiting preachers from many denominations to enrich our worship would please him.

As we entered this new century a statement was published to inspire the generations to come. It was written by Tom Fleming, who for over two decades led the way in shaping the Corporate Ministry into the living, vital entity it is. He said, simply:

I hope with all my heart that in the 21st Century, long after I have gone, Canonmills will quietly point the way forward for the church of the future; breaking down irreconcilable barriers, blazing the trail for the Corporate Ministry of ALL God's People, and being a witness for Christ as a caring and loving community, open to men and women of wide ranging backgrounds and beliefs and of no belief at all. For the last century, the church has been obsessed with bringing the world into the church, involving people in church organisations from the cradle to the grave. How many missions have had as their target, '...Taking the church into the world'! I have news for you. The church is IN the world for the church is people – people like

---

[127] A.C. Thomas, (ibid.), pp.32-35

us – and we spend 167 out of 168 hours of every week in the world. And the world – the world of everyday things, the world which Jesus came to save – is where Christ IS![128]

Two hundred years after our founding, we can look back with grateful thanks for the original minds, the courageous and groundbreaking work that has happened, quietly, within our midst. And we can honour that by giving thanks and carrying that pioneering spirit with us as we journey on.

---

[128] An extract from an address delivered in Canonmills by Tom Fleming, then Leader of the Corporate Ministry, on the first Sunday of 2000AD and reproduced in the 'Canonmills Magazine' February 2000

BIBLIOGRAPHY

- - - - -   An Account of the Proceedings of The Society for Propagating the Gospel at Home: their commencement, December 28 1798(sic.-1797) to May 16 1799   J. Ritchie (Edinburgh, 1799)

- - - - -   An Abridgment of the Acts of the General Assembly of the Church of Scotland From 1560-1830 Robert Buchanan (Edinburgh, 1831)

- - - - -   An Exhortation to Christian Forbearance and Union: Addressed to the Scotch Baptist Churches. Waugh & Innes (Edinburgh, 1834)

- - - - -   Acts of the General Assembly of The Church of Scotland 1638 – 1842 .Reprinted from the original edition, under the superintendence of The Church Law Society. The Edinburgh Printing and Publishing Company (Edinburgh, 1843)

- - - - -   "A Brief History of Dublin Street Baptist Church" in Bazaar Souvenir Booklet McLagan & Cumming Ltd. (Edinburgh, 1927)

- - - - -   The Concise Dictionary of National Biography: from the earliest times to 1785 Vol. II G-M. OUP (Oxford, 1993)

- - - - -   "Scotland and the Missionary Movement" http://www.schoolofministry.ac.nz/reformed/TCCH AP09.pdf

Baines, Annie M.   History of Dublin Street Baptist Church, Edinburgh 1885-1958 McLagan & Cumming Ltd. (Edinburgh, 1958)

Burleigh, J.H.S.   A Church History of Scotland OUP (London, 1960)

Chambers, Don   "Mission and Party in The Church of Scotland" Degree of Doctor of Philosophy (Selwyn College, University of Cambridge, 1971)

Cross, F.L. (Ed.)   The Oxford Dictionary of the Christian Church OUP (London, 1958)

Daiches, David   Sir Walter Scott and his World Thames & Hudson (London, 1971)

Drummond, A. L. & Bulloch, J.

The Scottish Church 1688 – 1843: The Age of the Moderates. The Saint Andrew Press (Edinburgh, 1973)

Escott, Harry

A History of Scottish Congregationalism The Congregational Union of Scotland (Glasgow, 1960)

Ewing, Greville (Ed.)

Missionary Magazine: A Periodical Monthly Publication intended as a repository of discussion, and intelligence respecting the progress of the Gospel throughout the world. Vol. I, No.i: Jul 1796; No.ii: Aug, 1796; No.iii: Sept, 1796; No.v: Oct, 1796; No.vii: Nov, 1796; Vol. VI, No. lvii: Feb, 1801; No.lviii: Mar, 1801; Vol VIII, No. lxxxvi: Jul, 1803

Fawcett, Rev. Arthur

"Scottish Lay Preachers in the Eighteenth Century" *Records of the Scottish Church History Society* The Very Rev. Hugh Watt; The Rev. Principal John H.S. Burleigh; The Rev. John A. Lamb; The Rev. A. Ian Dunlop & Rev. Thomas Maxwell (Eds.) Vol. XII; 1958

Findlay, James T.

The Secession in the North: The Story of an Old Seceder Presbytery 1688-1897. Lewis Smith & Son (Aberdeen, 1898)

Garrett, Leroy

"It Began in Scotland" *Restoration Review*: Vol. 19, No. 2; Feb. 1976 also at http://www.freedomsring.org/heritage/chap1.html

Gray, Nelson

"Greville Ewing, Architect of Scottish Congregationalism" *Degree of Doctor of Philosophy*, (University of Edinburgh, 1961)

Haldane, J. A.

Journal of a tour through the northern counties of Scotland and the Orkney Isles, in Autumn 1797: undertaken with a view to promote the knowledge of the Gospel of Jesus Christ. (---- ,1797)

Haldane, Alexander

The Lives of Robert Haldane of Airthrey, and of his Brother, James Alexander Haldane Esq. Third Edition. Hamilton, Adams, and Co. (London, 1853)

Henderson, G. D. (ed.)

The Scots Confession of 1560 with an introduction by G.D. Henderson, together with a rendering into modern English by the Rev. James Bulloch PhD. The Saint Andrew Press (Edinburgh, 1937)

Hill, Rowland

"A Series of Letters Occasioned by the Late Pastoral Admonition of the Church of Scotland, as also, Their Attempts to Suppress the Establishment of Sabbath Schools, Addressed to the Society for the Propagation of the Gospel at Home" J. Ritchie (Edinburgh, 1799)

Innes D.D., Rev Dr. William

Reasons for Separating from The Church of Scotland in a series of letters William Innes, Minister of the Gospel, Dundee. Chiefly addressed to his Christian Friends in that establishment. Chalmers, Ray & Co. (Dundee, 1804)

A Summary of the Leading Doctrines of the Word of God designed chiefly for the benefit of those who propose for the first time to join a Christian Church. Chalmers, Ray & Co. (Dundee, 1805)

Animadversions on a Late Pamphlet, entitled *The National Church Defended and Independency Refuted* by the Reverend James Smith, Dundee. With a view to point out some of the examples of false reasoning and misrepresentation, which occur in that publication. F. Ray (Dundee, 1806)

Sketches of Human Nature; or hints chiefly relating to the duties and difficulties that occur in the intercourse of Christians with one another, and with the world. (Edinburgh, 1807)

Remarks on Christian Union: or, An inquiry how far Christians are called to unite in things in which they are agreed, though there be other things in which they differ: in a letter to a friend. (Edinburgh, 1811)

Letter to the Editor of the *Christian Instructor* occasioned by a review of a volume entitled "Eugenio and Epenetus, &c." inserted in No. XVII of that work. Andrew Balfour (Edinburgh, 1812)

Domestic Religion: or an exposition of the precepts of Christianity regarding the duties of domestic life. 2nd Edition. Waugh & Innes (Edinburgh, 1822)

Christian Consolation Under Affliction illustrated in a short memorial of Mrs. Currie who died at Edinburgh, Dec. 13, 1827 Waugh & Innes (Edinburgh, 1828)

Origin and Permanence of Christian Joy: as connected with the doctrine of personal assurance. Waugh & Innes (Edinburgh, 1828)

The Power of the Presbyteries in a letter to a Presbyterian friend. R. Marshall (Edinburgh, 1832)

Reflections of an Enquirer on the Subject of Baptism Wm. Innes (Edinburgh, 1840)

The Infidel Catechised Wm. Innes (Edinburgh, ...)

Responsibility or Improve your Privileges Wm. Innes (Edinburgh, 1843)

"Sabbath" in A Tract for the Times MacLehose & Bryce (Glasgow, 1845)

Hints on Church Government from the experience of above half a century. Wm. Innes (Edinburgh, 1852)

Open Communion and Christian Forbearance in a letter to a mutual friend. Wm. Innes (Edinburgh, 1845)

Suggestions for Thoughtful but Sceptical Minds Wm. Innes   (Edinburgh, 1854)

Innes, William (Ed.)   Memoir of Martha Innes: Edinburgh, with extracts from her diary and letters. Compiled and Ed. by her husband. (London, 1844)

Jamieson, George   An Account of the Faith and Practices of the Scotch Baptists; with remarks on Scriptural Union; A view of the Faith and Order of the Primitive Churches of Christ… J. Neilson (Paisley, 1829)

Kirkland, William M.   "The Impact of the French Revolution on Scottish Religious Life and Thought with Special Reference to Thomas Chalmers, Robert Haldane and Neil Douglas" Degree of Doctor of Philosophy (University of Edinburgh, 1951)

Lovegrove, Deryck W.   "Lay leadership, establishment crisis and the disdain of the clergy" in The Rise of the Laity in Evangelical Protestantism Ed. Deryck W. Lovegrove. Routledge (London & New York, 2002)

McNaughton, W.D.   "A Few Historical Notes on Scottish Congregationalism"
http://www.westendcongregationalchurch.org/congregation.htm

The Scottish Congregational Ministry 1794-1993 Montgomery Litho (Glasgow, 1993)

Macpherson, Hector   Scotland's Battles for Spiritual Independence Oliver and Boyd (Edinburgh, 1905)

Mathieson, Wm. Law   The Awakening of Scotland: A History from 1747 to 1797 James MacLehose and Sons (Glasgow, 1910)

Church and Reform in Scotland: A History from 1797 to 1843. James MacLehose and Sons (Glasgow, 1916)

Meikle, Henry W.	Scotland and the French Revolution James MacLehose and Sons (Glasgow, 1912)
Paterson, Tom	"Parish of Stirling – V: Parochial Economy" http://www.web.ukonline.co.uk/tom.paterson/places/Sastirl05.htm
Raleigh, Sir Thomas	Annals of The Church of Scotland together with his own autobiographical notes and some reminiscences by Sir Harry R. Reichel. Humphrey Milford / OUP (London, 1921)
Richardson, Robert	Memoirs of Alexander Campbell Vol I (1868) Chap 10: "Religious Movement of the Haldanes – State of Religious Society in Scotland - Effects upon Alexander Campbell." http://www.mun.ca/rels/restmov/texts/rrichardson/mac/MAC110.HTM
Ross, James Rev.	A History of Congregational Independency in Scotland Esp. Part II: Later Independency in Scotland. James MacLehose and Sons (Glasgow, 1900)
Sands, Hon. Lord	"The Historical Origins of the Religious Divisions in Scotland" Records of The Scottish Church History Society W.J. Couper & Robert M'Kinlay (Ed.) Vol.III; 1929
Scott D.D., Hew	Fasti Ecclesiae Scoticanae: The Succession of Ministers in the Church of Scotland from the Reformation. New Edition Vol. I, Synod of Lothian and Tweedale. Oliver and Boyd (Edinburgh, 1915)
	Fasti Ecclesaie Scoticanae Vol III, Synod of Merse, Teviotdale, Dumfries and Galloway. Oliver and Boyd (Edinburgh, 1917)
Smith, George	The Life of William Carey: D.D. Shoemaker and Missionary, Professor of Sanskrit, Bengali and Marathi in the College of Fort William, Calcutta. 2nd Edition. (----,1887)
Stephen, W.	History of the Scottish Church Vol. II. David Douglas (Edinburgh, 1896)
Storrar, William F.	"From identity to liberation. Towards a new practical theological paradigm of Scottish Nationhood" Degree of Doctor of Philosophy, (University of Edinburgh, 1992)
Sutherland, John	The Life of Walter Scott: A Critical Biography Blackwell (Oxford, 1997)

Thomas, Alfred C.

Dr Innes and His Times a discourse delivered on the occasion of the death of the Rev. Dr. William Innes, D.D. in Charlotte Chapel, Edinburgh, on Sabbath Evening, March 11, 1855 with a brief sketch of his life. Wm. Innes (Edinburgh, 1855)

Vincent, Emma

"The Responses of Scottish Churchmen to the French Revolution, 1789 – 1802" in *The Scottish Historical Review,* Vol. LXXIII, 2 No. 196; Oct. 1994   pp.191-215

Yuille, Rev. Geo. (Ed.)

History of the Baptists in Scotland: From Pre-Reformation Times. Baptist Union Publications Committee (Glasgow, 1926)